GW00889701

The Ladder of Monks

—

GUIGO II THE CARTHUSIAN

The Ladder of Monks

translated by
Sr. Pascale-Dominique Nau

2012

Original Latin text : *Scala Claustralium*

is in public domain

ISBN: 978-1-291-03722-7

Introduction

Guigo II the Chartusian (1114 - c. 1193) was the ninth prior of the Grande Chartreuse. His *Ladder of Monks* is one of the great spiritual classics that has inspired the method of lectio divina –spiritual reading of the Holy Scriptures- since the early Middle Ages. In *Verbum Domine* n° 86, Pope Benedict XVI, quoting Origen's letter to Gregory, indicates one of Guigo's major sources:

the great Alexandrian theologian gave this advice: "Devote yourself to the lectio of the divine Scriptures; apply yourself to this with perseverance. Do your reading with the intent of believing in and pleasing God. If during the lectio you encounter a closed door, knock and it will be opened to you by that guardian of whom Jesus said, 'The gatekeeper will open it for him'. By applying yourself in this way to lectio divina, search diligently and with unshakable trust in God for the meaning of the divine Scriptures, which is hidden in great fullness within. You ought not, however, to be satisfied merely with knocking and seeking: to understand the things of God, what is absolutely necessary is oratio. For this reason, the Saviour told us not only: 'Seek and you will find', and 'Knock and it shall be opened to you', but also added, 'Ask and you shall receive'".

In Guigo's text, probably written toward 1150, we find the first systemization of the structure of lectio: reading-meditation-prayer-contemplation that has become the classical form of spiritual reading of Holy Scripture, constantly repeated throughout the centuries up to today. We find its influence, for example, in the reflection of Saint John of the Cross on lectio divina, and it provides the key for understanding William of Saint-Thierry's *On Contemplation*.

Guigo uses mostly imagery already present in the Bible and patristic literature. Two images are particularly important. First, his entire development is on the Gospel passage we just read in Origen, Mt 7:7

"Search, and you will find; knock, and the door will be opened for you".
Seek by reading,
*and you will **find** by **meditating**.*
Knock by praying,
*and you will **enter** by **contemplating**.*

Secondly, the image of the "mystic grape" that the Gospel offers to the soul to nourish it. The soul, beginning to read,

says to herself: This word will do me good! Concentrate yourself, o my heart, try to understand and, above all, to find this purity. O, how precious and desirable it must be, since it purifies those in whom it dwells and contains the promise of divine vision, of eternal life, since the Holy Scriptures unceasingly praise it!

The *work* then consists precisely in "pressing" this grape, to receive its nourishing juice. The verse Guigo uses as the example for his exposition is also from Matthew: "*Blessed are the pure of heart, for they will see God.*"

The following chapters deal with the result of good *lectio divina*: the coming of the Holy Spirit, and with difficulties generally encountered in prayer: the absence of the Bridegroom – this chapter is probably inspired by St. Bernard's writings on the subject; cf. for example in the *Commentary on the Song of Songs*, s. 32, 2; s. 51 and elsewhere–; the mutual rapport of reading, meditation, prayer and contemplation; and, finally, the four obstacles that lead to the loss of the grace of contemplation: *unavoidable necessity*, the *utility of a good work, human weakness,* and *worldly vanity* – at the beginning of *On Contemplation* William of Saint-Thierry (written between 1121 et 1124) offers a large development of this point.

Before his final salutation, Guigo closes the work with this prayer:

I pray the Lord to weaken today and remove tomorrow all that obstructs the soul's contemplation. May He lead us, from virtue to virtue, up to the top of the mysterious ladder, into the vision of God in Zion. There, His chosen will receive this divine contemplation not drop by drop or intermittently; on the contrary, they will always inundated by the stream of joy, possessing forever the bliss that no one can take from them, immutable peace, Peace in Him!

This is my wish and prayer for the readers of the present translation.

Sr. Pascale-Dominique

On the feast of SS. Peter and Paul, 29 June 2012

Warsaw, Poland

Introductory Letter
to His Beloved Brother Gervius

May the Lord be our joy!

My friendship for you is a debt because you loved me first; and I'm obliged to write to you since you incited me by writing to me first. So then, here are my thoughts about the spiritual exercises of the monks. You, having learned more from your experience than I have from my studies, will correct and judge them. For that reason, I offer the first fruits of my work to you: these first fruits of a young plant are due to you, who by means of a praiseworthy theft freed yourself from Pharaoh's slavery and entered into the ranks of those who fight in a delicious solitude. You skillfully pruned the wild plant and grafted it on a fruitful olive tree.

The Four degrees
of the Spiritual Exercises

One day, while working with my hands, I was reflecting on man's spiritual exercises, and suddenly I realized that there are four degrees: reading, meditation, prayer and contemplation. This is the ladder that leads monks from earth to heaven. Although it has few steps, it is very high and incredibly long. Its base is set on the earth, and its summit reaches above the clouds to penetrate the heights of heaven. The names, order and use of these steps differ. However, when we carefully study their properties, functions and hierarchy, they soon seem short and easy, because of their usefulness and sweetness.

Reading is the attentive study of the Holy Scriptures by an applied mind.

Meditation is the careful investigation of a hidden truth with the help of the intelligence.

Prayer is the elevation of the heart towards God, so that it separates itself from evil and reaches toward what is good.

Contemplation is the elevation of the ravished soul in God, where it savors the joys of eternity.

Now, after having defined these four steps, let us consider each one's particular role. The indescribable sweetness of the blessed life, is sought through *reading*, found in *meditation*, asked for in *prayer* and savored in *contemplation*. This is precisely what the Lord says: "Search, and you will find; knock, and the door will be opened for you" (Mt 7:7). Seek by reading, and you will find by meditating. Knock by praying, and you will enter by contemplating. I would like to say that reading brings the substantial food to the mouth; meditation grinds and chews it; prayer tastes it, and contemplation is the sweetness itself that delights and restores. Reading keeps to the rind, meditation enters into the marrow, prayer expresses the desire, but contemplation takes pleasure in savoring the sweetness obtained.

Reading

Here is an example that can help to make things clearer. In the Gospel, I read: *Blessed are the pure of heart, for they will see God.* The statement is short, but full of meaning and infinitely sweet. To the thirsting soul it offers a grape. The soul considers it and says to herself: This word will do me good! Concentrate yourself, o my heart, try to understand and, above all, to find this purity. O, how precious and desirable it must be, since it purifies those in whom it dwells and contains the promise of divine vision, of eternal life, since the Holy Scriptures unceasingly praise it! This is how the desire to understand invades the soul, who now takes hold of this mystic grape, slices it up, crushes

wicked soul. It comes only from God. The Lord has given to many the task of baptizing, to a few that of forgiving sins, but he kept this power for himself. Just as Saint John says: *Here is the one who baptizes,* we can say: Here is the only one who gives this savory wisdom and who can allow the soul to taste it. The text is offered to many people, but only a few receive this wisdom. The Lord infuses it into whom he wants and how he wants.

Prayer

The soul has understood. She could never have reached this precious knowledge, this sweet experience, with her own faculties; but the more she strains, the more God seems to elevate her. So, she humbles herself and takes refuge in prayer: Lord, whom only the pure of heart can see, I have sought, through reading and meditation, the true purity so that I may become able to know you at least a little. *I have sought your face, Lord; I have desired your adorable face* (Psa 26:8). *I have long meditated in my heart, and in my meditation a fire was set, the desire to know you evermore* (Psa 38:4).

When you broke the Bread of the Scriptures for me, I already knew you; but the more I know you, o my Lord, the more I want to know, not only in the rind of the letter, but in the reality of union. And this is the gift, Lord, that I implore, not for my merits, but for your mercy. It is true that I am an unworthy sinner, but don't *the little dogs eat the crumbs that fall from their master's table?* O God, grant to my anguished soul an advance of the promised inheritance, at least a drop of heavenly dew to still my thirst, for I am burning with love, Lord.

Contemplation

Through such ardent words, the soul inflames her desire and calls the Bridegroom with tender prayer. Then, the Bridegroom, whose gaze rests on the just and whose ears are so attentive to their prayers that he does not wait until they are fully expressed, suddenly interrupts this prayer: He comes to the longing soul, pours into her the heavenly dew and anoints her with precious perfumes; He restores the tired soul, nourishes the weak one, drenches the dried one; He makes her forget the earth and, detaching her from everything else by his presence, he marvelously strengthens, vivifies and inebriates her.

Certain crude acts so strongly keep the soul enchained through concupiscence that she loses her good sense and that the whole person becomes carnal. On the contrary, now, in this sublime contemplation, the bodily instincts are so entirely consumed and absorbed by the soul that the flesh no longer fights against the spirit, and the person becomes spiritual in every respect.

The Signs that Reveal
the Coming of the Holy Spirit

Lord, how can I discern the hour of this visit? What sign will permit me to recognize your coming? Are sighs and tears the messengers and witnesses of this consoling joy? This is a new simile, with an exceptional meaning! Indeed, what relation is there between consolation and sighing, between joy and tears? Can we really say that these are tears? Is this not rather the intimate dew poured overabundantly from above to purify a man's heart and that brims over? In baptism, the outer ablution signifies and operates the inner purification of the child; here, on the contrary, the intimate purification precedes the outer ablution and becomes manifest through it. O blessed tears, this new baptism of the soul extinguishes the fire of sins! *Blessed are you who weep, for you shall laugh* (Mt 5:5).

When the Bridegroom Leaves

Be quiet, my soul, you're talking too much.

It was good to be up there, with Peter and John, contemplating the Bridegroom's glory, staying with him for a long time, and –if he would have wanted– putting up not two or three tents but only one in which to dwell together in his joy! Yet, the Bridegroom is already exclaiming: *Let me leave, dawn is already coming.* You have received the luminous grace and the so strongly desired visit. Then he blesses you and, as the angel once did to Jacob, mortifies the nerve of your thigh (Gen 32:25.31); he changes your name from Jacob to Israel and thereafter seems to leave. The Bridegroom, desired for so long, quickly hides himself; the vision of the contemplation fades and its sweetness evaporates. Yet the Bridegroom remains present in your heart, constantly governing it.

Do not fear, o Bride, nor despair, and do not think that you're despised if, from time to time, the Bridegroom veils his face. All of this is for your good; his leaving is just as beneficial his coming. He comes for you and he leaves for you. He comes to console you and leaves to guard you, for fear that you might become proud because of his sweet presence. If the Bridegroom were always perceptibly present, would you not be tempted to despise your companions and believe that you deserve this presence, which is in fact a gift the Bridegroom grants to whom he wants and when he wants, and to which, finally, you have no right? The proverb says: "Familiarity engenders contempt." In order to avoid this disrespectful familiarity, he hides from your view. When he is absent, your desire for him grows; your desire makes you seek him with greater ardor, and your waiting makes your encounter more delightful.

Furthermore, if consolation were endless here on earth –although it is an enigma and a shadow in comparison with eternal glory–, we might believe that we're already in the eternal city and would seek the future city less. Oh, no! Let us not confound the exile with the homeland, and the advance with the inheritance.

The Bridegroom comes, bringing consolation and leaving desolated. He lets us taste a bit of his ineffable sweetness; but before it can penetrate us, he hides and leaves. Now, he does this in order to teach us to fly towards the Lord. Like an eagle, he extends his wings over us and pushes us to rise. And he says: You have tasted a bit of my sweetness. Do you want to be filled with it? Run, fly to my perfumes; lift up your hearts on high, to where I am at the right hand of the Father, where you will see me, no longer in figure or enigma but face to face, in the joy, full and complete, that no one can ever take away from you. The Bride of Christ understands this well. When the Bridegroom goes away, he is not far from you. You do not see him anymore, but he does not stop looking at you. You can never escape from his sight. His messengers, his angels, gaze on your life when he hides, and they will quickly accuse you if they see you lightheaded and impure. The Bridegroom is jealous, and if your soul admitted another love and tried to please someone else, he would leave you immediately to join the more faithful maidens. He is delicate, noble, rich, *the fairest of all the children of men*, and so he wants his bride to be very beautiful.

Consequently, if he sees a wrinkle or a spot in you, he will look away, because he cannot bear any impurity. Remain chaste, therefore, respectful and humble before him, and he will often visit you.

Carried away by my discourse, I have spoken too long. Yet how can I resist the impulse of such a fertile and pleasant subject? These beautiful things have captivated me. Now, let's sum them up for more clarity:

Reading is the basis. It provides the material and leads you to meditation.

Meditation is the careful search for what should be desired. It digs deep and reveals the hoped for treasure; but it is incapable of seizing it.

Prayer, directed with all its strength to the Lord, asks for the desirable treasure of contemplation.

Contemplation, finally, comes to recompense the work of her three sisters and inebriates with heavenly dew the soul thirsting for God.

Reading is then an outer exercise. It is the beginner's stage.

Meditation is an inner act of the mind. It is the stage of those who progress.

Prayer is the action of a soul filled with desire. This is the stage of those who long for God.

Contemplation is beyond all feeling and knowledge. It is the stage of the blessed.

Reading, Meditation, Prayer and Contemplation Sustain One Another

Reading, meditation, prayer and contemplation are so closely connected to one another and offer mutual help when necessary, that the former are useless without the latter and one never experiences the latter, or only very exceptionally, without going through the former. What good is it to use one's time reading the life and writings of Saints if, in pondering and reflection, we do not draw out their juice and make it our own by letting it descend into depths of the heart? Our readings will be useless, unless we take care to compare our lives with those of the saints and let ourselves be carried away by the interest of the reading rather than by the desire to imitate their example.

On the other hand, how can one stay on the right path and avoid errors or childishness?

How can we keep within the limits laid down by our Fathers without serious reading or learned education? For in the end we understand reading as instruction. Do people not commonly talk about: "—the book I read," although sometimes they received instruction from a master?

Likewise, the meditation on our duties will be vain, unless it is completed and strengthened by the prayer that obtains the grace to fulfill this duty, for *every exquisite gift, every perfect gift comes down from the Father of lights* (James 1:17), without which we cannot do anything. He works in us, but not entirely without us, because, says the Apostle (1 Co 3:9): *We are God's fellow workers*. He condescends to us as helpers of his works, and when he knocks on the door, he asks us to open the secret of our desire and consent.

The Savior asked for the Samaritan woman's consent, when he said: *Call your husband* (John 4:16) –that is to say: here is my grace; you, make use of your free will. He inspired her to prayer by saying: *If you knew the gift of God and*

34

who is the one who says to you, give me a drink, *certainly you would ask him for the living water* (John 4:10s). That woman, taught by meditation, says to herself within her heart: this water would be good for me; and, enflamed by burning desire, she began to pray: *Lord, give me this water so that I shall never* *again be thirsty and come to this well* (John 4:15). The word of God she heard invited her heart to meditate and pray. How would she have been brought to pray if meditation had not kindled her desire?

On the other hand, what would have been the use of meditation about the spiritual goods, if she couldn't have obtained through prayer? So, what is fruitful meditation? It develops in fervent prayer that obtains almost generally very sweet contemplation. Thus, without meditation is reading barren; without reading, meditation is full of errors; without meditation, prayer is lukewarm; without prayer, meditation is fruitless and vain. Prayer and devotion together obtain contemplation. On the contrary, for someone to reach contemplation without prayer would be very exceptional and miraculous. The Lord, whose power is infinite and whose mercy marks all his works, may well turn stones into children of Abraham, by forcing the hardhearted and rebellious to will good; he lavishes his grace, and takes the bull by the horns –as is commonly said–, when he suddenly and unexpectedly enters into the soul; *he* is the sovereign master. This is what he did to Paul and a few other chosen people. However, we must not expect such miracles and put God to the test. Let us do what is required of us: read, meditate on the divine law, and ask the Lord to look on our great misery and help our weakness. *Ask and you shall receive*, is what he himself says, *seek and you shall find; knock and the door will open.* Down here, in fact, *the kingdom of heaven suffers violence and the violent prevail* (Mt 7:7; 11:12).

Blessed is he who, detached from all creatures, constantly exercises himself, climbing the four steps! Happy is the man who sells everything in order to buy the field where the greatly desirable treasure of contemplation lies, and tastes sweetness of the Lord!

Applied in the first degree, cautious in the second, strong in the third, delighted at last, he climbs from one virtue to the next in his heart on the steps that lead up to the vision of the Lord in Zion. Blessed are those who can finally stop at the top, even for a moment, and say: I am enjoying the grace of the Lord; here, with Peter and John on the mountain, I contemplate his glory; with Jacob I share Rachel's caress. Yet, let this happy man be careful to not choose, alas, heavenly contemplation in the darkness of the abyss, divine vision in the midst of worldly vanities and impure fantasies of the flesh. The poor human soul is feeble; it cannot long endure the dazzling splendor of the truth. Therefore, he must carefully descend one or two degrees and then relax in one or the other, as he wishes or according to the grace he has, while always remaining as close to God as possible.

O how sad is the condition of human weakness! Here, reason and Scripture agree in telling us that perfection is reached through these four levels, and climbing them is the exercise the spiritual man must do. But who is following this path? Who is he, so that we may praise him? Many have ambitions but few go to the very end. May God grant us to be among this small number!

How the Soul Loses the Grace of Contemplation

Four obstacles may prevent us from climbing these steps: *unavoidable necessity*, the *utility of a good work*, *human weakness*, and *worldly vanity*. The first is excusable, the second acceptable, the third pitiful, and the fourth guilty.

Indeed, for the man who abandons his holy resolution to run after worldly vanity, it would be better to have never known the glory of God than to refuse it after having known it. How could such bad conduct be excused? To this faithless man, the Lord makes just reproaches: *What else could I have done for you?* (Isa 5:4). You were nothing, and I gave you being; you were sinful and enslaved by the devil, and I redeemed you; you were wandering through the world with the wicked, and lovingly I took you back, gave my grace and established my presence in you. I placed my dwelling in your heart, and you have despised my invitation, my love, my aim, and made all your plans far away, in order to run after to your desires.

O God, good, sweet and gentle, tender friend and wise counselor, strong help! Foolish and reckless is the man who rejects you and expels such a humble and compassionate guest from his heart! Unhappy and damnable exchange: he drives out his Creator to welcome impure and perverse thoughts; he opens the dear retreat close to the Holy Spirit, recently perfumed with celestial joys, to low and sinful thoughts; he profanes with adulterous desires what remains of the Bridegroom's visit. O dreadful impiety! Those ears, who have listened to the conversations that man cannot repeat, are now filled with lies and slander; the eyes cleansed by the holy tears now delight in vanity; those lips, that have just stopped singing the divine epithalamium and ardent songs of love that united the Bridegroom and the Bride in the mystical cellar, now speak vanity, deceit and slander. O Lord, save us from such falls! Yet, if human weakness made you fall unfortunately, o fragile soul, do not despair. No, never despair, but run to the noble doctor who raises the poor from the dust, and lifts the needy from the dung heap (Psa 112:7). He does not want the death of the sinner. He will care for you and heal you.

Conclusion

I have to bring my letter to a close. I pray the Lord to weaken today and remove tomorrow all that obstructs the soul's contemplation. May He lead us, from virtue to virtue, up to the top of the mysterious ladder, into the vision of God in Zion. There, His chosen will receive this divine contemplation not drop by drop or intermittently; on the contrary, they will always inundated by the stream of joy, possessing forever the bliss that no one can take from them, immutable peace, Peace in Him!

O Gervius, my brother, when by the grace of the Lord you will have reached the top of this mysterious ladder, remember me and, in your happiness, pray for me.

In this way one servant draws another to himself, and whoever hears says, *Come!*

Contents

36856399R00028